Coffee Time

Mary Njeri Kinyanjui

Langaa Research & Publishing CIG
Mankon, Bamenda

Publisher:

Langaa RPCIG
Langaa Research & Publishing Common Initiative Group
P.O. Box 902 Mankon
Bamenda
North West Region
Cameroon
Langaagrp@gmail.com
www.langaa-rpcig.net

Distributed in and outside N. America by African Books Collective
orders@africanbookscollective.com
www.africanbookscollective.com

ISBN: 9956-762-90-3

DISCLAIMER
All views expressed in this publication are those of the author and do
not necessarily reflect the views of Langaa RPCIG.

Dedication

This book is dedicated to the family of Ngomi Mwembu

Coffee time mesmerises me in Europe. People in Europe take it seriously. Each time I meet someone new, the conversation ends with an offer for coffee. What makes this frothy dark brown liquid so important in this part of the world? In Europe, Coffee drinking is common. It takes place in homes, offices and in *cafés*. It is taken for varied reasons: for leisure, to spur mental alertness, to ease digestion, to punctuate conversation, to break the ice, to extend a welcoming hand, fill business deal gaps or simply to satiate addiction.

Since coffee is part of office, church, school and shopping mall life, the coffee vending machine has become an important piece of equipment. What one needs to do is to slot some coins into the machine, select a number and the machine dispenses a ready cup of coffee. The human traffic to the coffee machine never ceases. Designer label coffee makers and street coffee makers compete for the same market. Coffee is made in different styles to elicit different tastes. There is *un la caffè crème, caffè laitte, cappuccino, mocca, expresso* and off course Irish coffee that is mixed with vodka.

While coffee seems to be the magic drink that animates – Europe especially, Coffee time does not excite me. It reminds me of my childhood experiences. In the village, peasants work on coffee farms for many hours but do not experience the thrill that their product elicits in the developed world.

In the village, the young and the old are harassed during coffee time. They wake up early and sleep late. They travel long distances to the farm or to the factory. While picking coffee, they do not take coffee breaks or lunch breaks. The objective is to clear the coffee picking job first and then take tea and food later. During coffee time, the peasants are on a day's fast. They do not even drink water or take food. They put much time and energy in the coffee work, yet they remain poor. Development theory calls them ignorant peasants and people without agency awaiting modernisation and empowerment. This is in dire contrast with international companies trading in coffee such as Nestle and Starbucks. These are global economic leaders with patents protecting their coffee.

I grew up in a rural small scale farm. All my parents and relatives are small scale coffee farmers. My paternal grandfather was a small scale coffee farmer. He spent most of his time tending coffee bushes. He had learnt the skill on the job in a *muthungu's* (European) coffee farm in Thika. He remembers his experience at the *muthungu's* coffee farm with mixed feelings. Workers lived in tiny round mud walled grass thatched huts arranged in neat rows and separated from each other by a small space. A person in one hut could clearly capture the conversation in a neighbour's house. It was difficult to keep family secrets. If a family had a quarrel, the neighbours would know. Individuals could tell what the next door family was cooking. News would easily spread about a family that always cooked the same type of food. The workers fetched water from a common pool and shared toilets and bathrooms. To avoid wastage of water and to keep water costs low, the water was rationed. Women would queue to fetch water. AS they did this, they caught up with news in the camp. They would know whose husband had been beaten by the *nyabara* (foreman), the man who had been insulted, which girls in the camp were pregnant or the recent social adventures of the *muthungu*.

Clothes were hung on common cloth lines and people would easily know the home where children had tattered clothes or new clothes. Children who were not old enough to join their families in the farm would play games outside the huts. The older ones would attend a local primary school to pass time and grow into adults since hardly any quality teaching took place. The children's dreams and visions were narrow. Their life's line graph was clearly drawn. They had no other place to go to other than join their parents as workers in the *muthungu* farm.

Work began at six o'clock in the morning and ended at six o'clock in the evening. Each worker was allocated a daily portion of land to till or coffee bushes to prune by the *nyabara*. The *nyabara* would measure the daily portion of work using footsteps for each individual worker. The workers worked at the same pace and speed.

The *nyabaras* were hated supervisors. They were ruthless and no nonsense persons. They wore a stern face, looked at people with a squint and rarely smiled. They had little, if any training, in human resource management. They looked for trouble and mistakes which they always found.

My grandfather remembers an incident where one of the workers injured his hand and cried out loudly as blood gushed from the cut. Instead of the *nyabara* taking him for medical attention, he told him: "You lazy bone! When did you last eat meat? Cut off that hanging piece of flesh and use it to make stew for use with your *ugali* (maize meal) in the evening." One worker who came to his colleague's help was given a through beating and ordered to go back to work. The injured man bled until he collapsed. It was then that the *nyabara* ordered some three men to put him on a handcart and take him to hospital. He never reached the hospital. He expired on the way. He was one of the longest serving workers in the farm and nobody knew where he came from. His remains were buried in the municipal cemetery as a vagabond.

Nyabaras were hated and feared. They were the mediators between the workers and the *muthungu*. The *muthungu* would also make rounds on horseback to see how work was going on and receive reports about workers from the *nyabara*. He enjoyed the horse ride as much as he admired his coffee bushes full of berries. He would shout to the *nyabara* and ask him questions like: "What is that red eyed good for nothing boy doing? Did he not have breakfast at all? Ask him to put in more effort."

After the rounds, the *muthungu* would sit at the porch and sip some dark coffee. Sometimes white farmers from neighbouring farms would also visit and share the coffee. They would laugh loudly and play games which were unknown to my grandfather. Woe to my grandfather if the *nyabara* spotted him staring at the whites. He would loss his salary for it. He had to keep his eyes on the coffee bush lest he lost his day's pay.

My grandfather dreaded the job but had to do it. He needed money to pay tax, pay his son's school fees and to feed his family. With the job, he was able to pay the tax and did not have to play hide and seek to escape arrest. He used to remember how he would rush into the bush at the sound of the police Landover. The vehicle roared and hissed as it went up the hills and down the valleys. Men in drinking halls at the shopping centres would scamper for safety at the noise because they feared spending time at the small, dark and smelly police cells in Gatundu or Thika that harboured drunkards, criminals and tax defaulters. The workers toiled from morning to evening. The taxes introduced by the *muthungu* government forced them to work so that they could pay tax.

The greatest thing that independence bestowed on my

grandfather and other small scale farmers was the authority to grow coffee. He would tell us that before independence, only the *muthungu* was allowed by law to do so. Africans were not allowed to grow the crop. It was feared that diseased African coffee would infect that of the *muthungu*. Independence meant that my grandfather could now work on his coffee farm. He would not leave home to seek employment at the *muthungu* farm in Thika again. He was his own boss and he took pride in it.

Coffee was close to his heart. The cow that gave him milk was bought with proceeds from coffee. His long dark *kabutis* (winter coats) bought in a second hand market in Thika were renewed after every coffee payment. He was able to pay the *muthungu* doctor who managed his chest illness with money from coffee. He paid fees for his grandchildren from coffee earnings. That is why the coffee tree was very important to him.

He knew each of his coffee trees. He sensed when the bushes needed pruning by the look of the branches. He knew when it was time to spray them although he never kept a calendar. Sadly, he died of undefined chest illness. An illness which could have been caused by the chemicals he used to spray the coffee. I remember he would contract a bad cough after spraying the coffee plant or when the coffee plant was flowering.

He is not the only one who succumbed to a chest illness in my village. My uncle and my aunt who also used to spend many hours on the coffee farm also succumbed to similar illnesses. My uncle was a reputable coffee farmer. He had learnt coffee management techniques from an agricultural college. He applied the skills he had learnt to the letter. His coffee was always ranked number one. He was a model farmer to many peasant farmers. When the sun would go down and bright orange rays were in the horizon, he would be on the farm pruning the trees and supporting the branches which were laden with berries lest they broke. He would leave the farm when it was dark. His chest problem was no different from that of my grandfather. He would wheeze and cough but undeterred, he continued working on the farm until he succumbed.

My aunt did not have a coffee farm of her own but worked tirelessly on her father's coffee farm. Being a single mother, she had to work extra hard on her father's farm. According to custom, a woman works on her husband's farm if married or her father's farm if unmarried. She diligently weeded the coffee farm, applied fertilizer, thinned and sprayed the coffee crop. Once she resorted to weeding, she would not rest until she had weeded around ten coffee bushes. She would strategically *kuruga* (a special way of removing weeds on the coffee farm). Holding the *ruhiu* with both hands, the right hand holding the handle and the left one placed in the middle, she would horizontally move the *ruhiu* below the surface and occasionally release the left hand and with it remove the weeds. She would shake the weeds to remove soil and throw them behind her. The movement of her hands would go with the movement of her hips. From above, it looked as if she was performing a dance. The movement of her body as she weeded rhymed with the song *Ave Maria* which she loved to sing at the top of her voice.

Ave Ave Ave Maria
Mwana wa Maria ndamutiga.
(Maria never abandons her child)
Akairaga nake hindi ciothe.

(She is always by her children side)
Angihingirio aikaraga nake moromo.
In case the house is full, she stays with the child at the
door
Ave Ave Ave Maria

As she sang, the space she was weeding would continue to expand. She would look behind proudly and laud herself for a job well done. This signalled that it was time for her to leave the coffee farm and attend to other household chores.

My aunt's compound did not have elaborate architecture and was on the southern bank ridge of River Chania. The compound had three rectangular houses made of mud and wood and roofed with iron sheets. These houses were considered modern because they had replaced the traditional round mud and grass thatched huts. My grandfather's house separated my aunt's house from my grandmother's. My grandmother's house was to the right and my aunt's house was to left. In between were open spaces which were used for leisure and for household chores.

The caked mud bricks on the houses had separated with time and created small openings. At the crack of dawn, cocks would crow, as a chilling breeze passed through the holes. The breeze was the morning wake-up call that made one cling tightly to their blankets. As the morning wore on and darkness gave way to light, the holes would let in bright yellow sun rays. They would make everything on their path look yellow including the mixture of white milk and water boiling on the fire.

My aunt's house was divided into three rooms. Her bedroom and that of her two daughters' were separated by an open space that doubled up as a resting place, a shower room and store for her farm produce. One room in my grandfather's house served as a kitchen and the family room. There was a special position for her in the kitchen. It was strategically located close to the cooking pots, the utensils tray and the water point. This ensured that all the things she needed while cooking were within reach. Above her sitting position was the front face of the *itaara* (the suspended wood drying tray). When she needed firewood, all she had to do was stand up and get it from the *itaara*. A fire place consisting of three stones was located in the middle of the room.

When she came home from the farm, she made lunch with a lot of ease. She would pull out the smouldering wood she had covered with ashes in the morning to preserve fire and pile thin pieces of wood and some dry leaves over it. She would blow onto the arrangement three or four times and a bright flame would emerge. She would place a *sufuria* (pan) on fire, put some cooking fat in it, add some sliced onions, drop in sliced tomatoes after the onions had become brown and put in scoops of some previously boiled *Githeri* (a mixture of maize and beans). She would stir the mixture for some minutes and then add water and salt. The noise from the bubbling *githeri* would be dwarfed by the fireside stories. When the food was ready, she would hold the hot *sufuria* with bare hands and quickly remove it from the fire and call her children who were waiting for the food in the yard.

She would serve equal portions for her daughters. The son would get slightly more than the girls. While serving, she would ask them how they had spent their day, talk to them about their future life and tell them about the relationship between hard work and eating. "If you do not work hard there will be no food for you," she would say. She served her children *githeri* from Monday to Monday.

Her daughters would tell her about the experiences they had at the river while fetching water with other girls. The boy would tell her about his experience with the animals in the field. How the cow went mad and broke the fence and ran into the neighbour's farm and ate her maize.

My aunt adjusted to life according to the farming seasons. She was very dynamic. During the coffee manuring season, she would wake up early in the morning. With a shovel in hand, she would go to the cowshed and dig deep into the green manure that the cows had trodden on for months. She would lift the hoe high up and then sink it deep into the heap of the green manure. She would shake the hoe to free it of the sticky chunk of weeds cemented by cow dung and hardened by the trampling of the cow. She would then throw the chunk of loose manure behind her into a pile. As she lifted the hoe, she would take a deep breath and then breathe out after hitting the ground. On and on she went until all the manure was loosened up and removed from the cow shed.

She would then begin the trips of carrying manure up the hill to the coffee plot. She would put the manure in a sack, strap the sack using a rope and hoist it onto her back, ready to climb the hill as she sang her favourite song: *Ave Maria*. On reaching the plot, she would drop her load, take a deep breath and then sprinkle the green manure into small heaps close to the coffee tree. It was the responsibility of children to spread out the manure and bury it into the soil.

Spraying coffee was mostly done by men. The women fetched water in advance to mix the chemicals. Down the hill she would rush with a *mutungi* (jerry can) on her back. Like a beast of burden, she made numerous trips to the small river to fill up the drums. When the drums were full, she would

9

move on and join the men in spraying. She had more muscle than them and she would operate the pressure pump while the men dragged the pipes. She seemed to enjoy pushing the pump up and down with sweat streaming down her face as she sang her beloved song *Ave Maria*.

My aunt knew how to keep everyone engaged during coffee harvesting. She would tell stories that ensured that no one was left behind. If one was left behind they would never catch up. After the harvesting, she would join the others for the weighing and cleaning. The weighing of coffee was critical. It revealed one's effort in the picking process. The measuring was done in *Ndebes* (tin cans) which weighed about five kilograms. For each *ndebe,* one was paid five Kenya Shillings. After weighing, all the coffee was heaped together and then cleaned. The heap would rise at the pouring of each *ndebe* to the extent that the people on one side could not see those on the other side.

The cleaning started from the fringes of the heap to the interior. The cleaning involved the removal of beans that were dry known as *mbuni*, over-ripened ones and the green ones that were not yet ripe. After cleaning, the coffee would be put in sacks ready for transportation to the factory. Women, girls and boys would traverse hills and valleys as they carried the heavy sacks of coffee to the factory after harvest. The factory was about seven kilometres away.

My aunt was very active in church. She was a member of St Anne and the Catholic Woman Association (CWA). Apart from her work on the farm, the next important thing in her life was the church. She spent the little money she had on church contributions. She was never left behind during offerings on Sunday masses. She liked the offertory song:

Twarehe matega mbere yaku we mwathani.
We bring you these offerings
Ni thithino ya wira wa moko maitu.
Sweat from the work of our hands
Mwathani moe no marathime
Lord take and bless
waheana na kameni muigana na ucio
If you give a small portion the blessings will equally be
small
mwathani moe no marathime.
Lord take and bless
*Waheana na giitirira Muigana no ucio Mwathani moe no
marathime*
If you give a big portion the blessings will equally be large
Mwathani moe no marathime
Lord take and bless

She would sing the song with a lot of energy as she walked to the altar to give her offerings. Afterwards, she would take her seat and pensively stare at the altar! What was crossing her mind? Was she wondering about the size of her portion of blessings? Or when her blessings would come?

The coffee job was not an easy one but she had to do it anyway. Day in day out, with little protective cloth, she worked on the coffee farm. She over exerted herself. Her hard work earned her praise and with time people forgot that she had defied tradition by remaining unmarried. She never showed fatigue. She was the envy of everyone because of how hard she worked. She developed a bad chest and finally succumbed to death.

In spite of all the time she had devoted to hard work, prayer and church activities, she was buried like a *kafiri* (nonbeliever). The priest was not available to say mass during her funeral. No apology or explanation was given. A priest only presides over a funeral mass of someone who has fulfilled all the church obligations and has lived a good Christian life. My aunt did not get this honour of having a priest officiate at her funeral mass.

The funeral was well attended. Members of St Anne came in large numbers dressed in white. They described my aunt as a good Christian who was very concerned with the church growth. She had a very authoritative voice which commanded everyone to take action. The leader of the *Mwaki* (Small Christian Community organised at the village level) described my aunt as a very committed member. She always mobilised people into action like cleaning the church and leading in prayers. She always led others in doing *kibaruas* (casual work on farms) for fundraising for church activities. She was also a member of Kolping, an organisation that espoused self-reliance. The CWA and St Anne members worked hard to fill the grave with soil and put her to her final resting place as they sang the song of St. Monica. They mourned my aunt, the unsung heroine of faith and work who had overcome her two main limitations of lack of education and unmarried status through hard work and commitment to the Christian faith.

After reading too many theories of development, underdevelopment and alleviating poverty, I have come to the conclusion that the development problem lies in the paradox of coffee time. My grandfather, uncle and aunt lived it. When one quietly sips a hot cup of coffee on a cold winter day at Starbucks or an ordinary coffee house in a London, Paris or Berlin back street, one does not take into consideration that it is a product of many hours of undervalued work of men and women like my grandfather, uncle and aunt in some part of Africa. Luckily, unlike petro consumers, those of coffee do not complain of the high prices or ask for subsidies to meet their expenses of coffee or tea even in winter. States can therefore choose to ignore market politics surrounding the marketing of tea and coffee in international markets.

Coffee farmers in Africa work and trade in distorted markets characterized by injustices in structure and form not only in prices but also in the value attached to commodities as well as the way they are organized. They have no intellectual property rights to the coffee they produce. Since independence, little has been done to restructure the skewed coffee trade or reconfigure it in a manner that will restore trade justice. In spite of the economic reforms of the 1990s, coffee producers are still left at the vagaries of the world market and little has been done to energize their bargaining power.

This coffee paradox disturbed me very much while pursuing my PhD at Cambridge University. I could not tell why development theory talked about modernisation, Rostow's stages of development, ignorant peasants, petty producers and informal sector underdevelopment while the peasant's products like coffee were sold in supermarkets as decaffeinated coffee from Germany, or Nescafe a product of Nestle. No attempts were made to explain where they originated from.

In the midst of confusion and reading theories that did not make sense to me and Rowstow's stages of economic growth, the paradox of coffee time became more complex. Who was the referee or midwife to ensure that the right path is followed from take off stage to the next stage? I questioned Rowstow's stage of High Mass Consumption as I sipped hot chocolate from the vending machine downstairs: how much can an individual consume in one sitting? Why is development measured in terms of consumption? Development is the state where human life is respected and human relationships honoured. How will people like my aunt move from take off stage to the stage of high mass consumption? A stage where each family will own two cars, each child have a room to themselves and eat a three course meal every day? The theories of development and episodes of disempowered peasants are written down by people who are kept awake by coffee.

Coffee time was the busiest time in my life. The day began early. As early as five o'clock in the morning. My mum always made hot tea to begin the day. I had to drink it before I set off for the coffee farm. The journey to the farm was long. It took an hour and half of walking up down the hills and crossing three rivers in-between. On arrival at the farm, I would take a row of coffee bushes to begin picking the coffee berries. The bushes were laden with red berries. The berries were picked one by one. I hung a small bag on my shoulder to put in the berries. The cold and sticky berries would pass through my tender fingers as I counted eachof them until I lost count. In no time, I would fill the container and empty it into a sack.

"Today I must fill four *Ndebes*" I would tell myself. "This is where my school fees comes from, as well as my clothes and food." My geography teacher used to say that Kenya earns foreign exchange from the coffee proceeds.

I encountered many things while picking coffee. From a chameleon climbing on my arm to sharp stings by insects or bites by spiders. I would scream loudly.

My father from the other end would shout: "What is it this time"?

I would reply, "a chameleon!"

He would then answer, "do not be a coward, a chameleon will not bite you!"

When stung by an insect, my aunt from far would intervene: "A woman should learn to bear pain. You scream because of chameleons. You run away because of spiders and now just a small sting makes you scream again. What a coward! You should be strong my child. Hard times await you. Do you know how much pain awaits you in future? Pain is what a woman wakes up to and sleeps up to. A woman was condemned to pain because of misleading Adam into eating the forbidden fruit."

She would continue: "You denied us the celebrations that come with traditional initiation rites. All girls of your age put up with so many things. Some of them are already mothers."

I felt like telling her: "Stop! I have chosen a different path. School first. Do you want me to drop out of school like the rest of the girls? I am looking for something deeper."

My father would interject: "What are you telling her? She has to learn both ways. She has to learn to use her hands and her brains."

My aunt would reply: "I want her to be educated but also

be a woman. A woman who never shows fatigue, a woman who wakes up early in the morning and prepares breakfast for her family, milks the cows, opens the chicken pen and then leaves for the farm. I want her to have her own children, take care of them, take care of her husband's property and do her office job. Don't think that I want her to be like me- *mundu wa thururu* (someone who spends the day digging on the farm). I want her to be good in both worlds. I know I am disadvantaged because I did not go to school. If I had stayed on, I would have a watch on my hand and wear tights rather than *marinda* (pleated dress). I would have other people wait on me. I would have gone far and wide with education. Given the chance again I would study and go to *Ruraya* (abroad) to study there."

My father would reply: "Maturity is not determined by traditional initiation rites of passage only. Age also determines it. My daughter has not stopped growing older."

"But she does not have a girlfriend of her age. Don't you think this is strange? I always see her walk alone or with boys," My aunt would reply.

"I believe that in school, she has friends. Besides, she also has her brothers and sisters to give her company."

"She has to be tough. We a living in a ruthless world. Only tough people can navigate around this," my aunt would reply.

Yes! I had got to be tough. I was being judged from many angles. I had to show that secondary education had not destroyed the woman in me. I had to show that although I missed the traditional initiation rites, I was not a coward. I could do all the things that women do with ease. I had to stand by that decision I made and do things exceptionally well to prove to my aunt that being a woman was not determined by traditional initiation rites. Going to school was important. In school one would learn about adolescence, puberty, personal hygiene, health care, how to wash babies, wash and iron clothes and cook great meals.

Yes! I had to be tough in order to succeed. I had a point to make that high school education had not messed me up. I was skilled at using my hands as well as brain. I was still a village girl at heart. I had to show this by picking coffee like everybody else.

I remembered a village girl who had participated in the traditional initiation rites and became a family celebrity after admission to high school. She would not carry her own box from the bus stop. After school, her mother would wait for her, pick up her box, tie it with a rope, hoist it on her back and take it home while the school girl gracefully walked behind her. The village boys would walk behind her and imitate her walking style. The girl never ate *Githeri* (a mixture of maize and beans), food that we were all used to in the village. Her dish was rice and cabbage. She never washed her clothes. Her mother would always leave work early to go and cook for her.

The girl never worked on the farm. At nine o'clock in the morning, when her peers were already in the farm picking coffee, she would be seen sitting at the front of her mother's house basking in the sunshine, reading a book or waiting for her lunch. Sometimes she would be heard shouting out to her mother in the coffee farm: "Mother! Mother! Where did you keep the sugar? I cannot find it." Instead of the mother directing her where to locate the sugar, she would rush back to show her. When she completed her four years in high school, she never came back to the village. She got married. Nobody ever talked of her again. I am sure my aunt did not want me to behave like this girl.

The village boys were advantaged. They had their own small houses. They rarely worked on the farm. In the late afternoon, they would stroll along the village paths to while-away time. Girls were attracted to them. Some of the village girls easily fell for their amorous tricks. A boy would offer to privately coach a girl in science subjects. In the process of private coaching, one girl after another would become pregnant. I remember, when one girl reported that she had been made pregnant by a secondary school village boy, the mother of the boy confronted her and told her that she had asked for it. She was accused of interfering with the boy's prospects of getting a good job in the city.

Sometimes, the boy who had done this would be taken to the village *baraza* (Chief's meeting) where the issue was discussed. The *baraza* comprised the chief, five village elders and stakeholders in the matter who included the girl's mother and aunt.

The chief would take a deep breath, clear his throat and announce the reason for the *baraza*. The announcement would take the following thread:

"This *baraza* has been called because Mzee Kamau says that someone has broken his goat's leg. That person is the son of Mzee Njorogore. Son of Mzee Njoroge, do you take responsibility?"

The boy would stand up and reply: "No. I have not done such a thing. I have never been with her. I am not the type to walk around with dirty village girls like her. No! No! It is not me. It cannot be me. After all she is always with Kimani."

Kimani would stand up and address the girl. "Gathoni! You mean you have been cheating on me. After I was with you, you ended up with someone else?"

A third boy would shoot up: "Gathoni, what do you mean? How could you do this to me? After all the assurances you have been giving me, you were also going out with my friends? What a shame!"

"Stop it!"Gathoni's mother would weigh in. "You son of Njoroge, didn't you offer to be giving remedial lessons in Science to Gathoni so that she would do well in her exams and join secondary school like you? I have not seen Gathoni with any other man in her life!"

"No. That is not true," Kimani would answer. "Although Gathoni is my friend, it appears she has been playing games on the three of us. *Wazee* (village elders) do you think this girl is telling the truth?"

A dejected and humiliated Gathoni would bend in shame and burst into tears. She could not bear the humiliation.

"Are you sure that none of you is responsible for the pregnancy?" The chief would ask the suspected boys present.

"We are not responsible!" They would reply in unison.

Amidst sobs, Gathoni would try to make her point but all the odds against her, she would take off.

Her father would stand up and address her mother: "You woman. I have always told you to teach good morals to your daughter. Look at the embarrassment she has brought me. Three men fighting for her. Shame on you woman! What kind mother are you!?"

The father would walk out of the meeting in anger. There being no one to prosecute, the chief would dismiss the *baraza*.

Secondary school boys and village girls' stories never ended. Their cases used to occupy a lot of the chief's time. Chiku was a very intelligent girl. She was a potential secondary school girl. The teachers were very happy with her performance and were sure that she would join a good high school. During August holidays, high school boys would offer her free private coaching. One of her coaches impregnated her. The village boy responsible did not want to be taken to the village *baraza*. He somehow liked the girl and sympathized with her state. He was very concerned that she would not go to high school as she had intended. He also feared his father very much and did not want to embarrass him in a village *baraza*. He sought advice from a friend who told him not deny the pregnancy but say that he was not ready for marriage at the time. He asked the boy to ask the girl to name the child after his father if it was a boy or his mother if it was a girl, according to custom.

Since the boy did not want to involve the father, he asked his friend to act as the go between. His friend was senior in age and went as the emissary to the girl's father. The two organised that the boy should steal his father's goat to take to the girl's father as sign of his good intentions. At night, the boy secretly hid one of the goats and took it to his friend's house and informed the parents that the goat was being brought because it needed a he goat. He would come for it in the morning at around eleven o'clock in the morning. His friend's parents did not think it was strange because the families used to exchange goats whenever they needed to change breeds.

At eleven o'clock, the two friends took the goat to the girl's father. They found the father warming under the late morning sun after he had had his breakfast. He was surprised to see two young men with a goat. After the usual greetings, the boy's friend announced the reason for their visit.

"I am sure you are surprised to see us here with a goat this morning in your house," he began. "Karimi wants to be part of your family. That is why he has brought this goat. He has broken Ciku's leg and wants to marry her after he completes school and gets a job. He brings you this goat as sign of good relationship."

Chiku's father was angry and confused. "What kind of news do you bear in a morning? Ciku my daughter, is pregnant? No! It cannot be."

He stood up, picked his walking stick and aimed it at the guilty party. "Karimi, how dare you do this to my daughter?"

Without warning, the walking stick landed on the guilty boy's head? Before a stool followed suit, the two boys took off with maximum speed, leaving the goat behind. The matter landed in the Chief's *baraza*. After much deliberation, it was decided the guilty boy should foot the baby's upkeep and that the girl should go back to school.

All these experiences made me wary and cautious in my day to day activities. I resolved not to fall victim to such traps but work hard in school and get a job in town. In the meantime however, coffee work had to proceed as usual. I had to fill my *ndebe*. I had to weigh each *ndebe*. The price for each *ndebe* was one Kenya shilling and fifty cents. Most of us took home between three and four shillings. This money was enough to buy a pen and few goodies that pleased both children and young adults. It could also be used to buy sugar, salt and toiletries. It was hardly enough but it sufficed. I had to participate in the coffee berry cleaning exercise. Not much talking took place during this phase. Everyone was fatigued and the mouths were dry. Once in a while someone would crack a joke but the laughing spell would be short lived. Slowly we all delved into cleaning the coffee in a squatting position. The clean berries would be put in sacks ready for taking to the factory.

After this, I had to embark on the journey to take the coffee to the factory. The journey and stay in the factory was arduous. It comprised climbing hills and going down valleys to factories which were strategically located near rivers. This is because a lot of water was used in the first stage of coffee processing. The next three days would be spent queuing at the factory waiting for coffee to be weighed before the first stage processing in preparation for the coffee's journey to distant places overseas.

The factory operatives were mean looking guys. They would sample a few sacks from the piles to find out whether the coffee was cleaned properly. If the coffee in two of the selected sacks was dirty, they would order one to remove it from the sacks and embark on cleaning it again. It would take time before they came back on another round to find out whether the coffee was now clean. If the coffee was clean, the operative would provide a coloured piece of paper to show the weighing clerk. Armed with the coloured piece of paper, one would join the weighing queue.

With the little energy remaining, we spent time pulling and pushing sacks of coffee until it was our turn to weigh. There were no seats on the queue and we had to stand all along. We could not sit on the coffee sacks because the operatives would accuse us of pressing the berries. There were no trolleys to push or pull the sacks and this meant that all sacks had to be moved by hands. The sacks had to be lifted by hand onto the big Avery weighing machine. The Avery machine took three sacks of coffee at a time. After all the sacks were weighed, the clerks would issue a receipt showing the number of kilograms. The number of Kilograms for the season would be aggregated and payment made on the basis of the cumulated weights. There was a waiting period before payments were made. Payments were made in instalments to the head of the family who in most cases was the man. Women and children's involvement in that coffee season ended immediately after weighing.

When the announcements of payments were made, men would travel to Thika and Gatundu towns to collect the payment. Some would come home very disappointed because of the low payments as the coffee earnings were not equal to the effort put during coffee time. Some farmers would quarrel the clerks upon seeing the bank statement. Some would be seen scratching their heads while others talked to themselves at the counter. They never understood why after putting in so much effort the, coffee pay was so little.

One day, I accompanied my father to the bank. When he received the statement, he started talking to himself, and said *"uyu ni guo wira uria ndirarutite kimera kiu giothe. Thukuru Nguri ha na ki?, Runi rukurihwo na ki?. Ndirarutire wira wa buri biu?* "Is this the money for all the work on the coffee farm for the last season? What will I pay the school fees with? How will I service the loan? Does is it mean all the work was a loss?"

The cashier looked at him with pity and told him: "Old man, that is how it is. Move and give way for the next person on the queue.". My father moved and walked away murmuring. He headed to his favourite pub - Brilliant - where he ordered a *Tusker* for himself and a *Fanta* for me. After taking one, he accompanied me to school where he was at pain explaining to the headmistress why he was not able to pay the term's fees in full. The headmistress looked at him and told him that she was sorry about the experience but full fees had to be paid. He was given a month to submit the balance.

Today, as I sit at the delegate's lounge at *Plais de Nations* having my usual *chocolat chaud* and watching delegates enjoying their hot cups of coffee after heated debates perhaps on poverty and economy, the SMS beep on my cell phone goes on. The message is from my father. He wants me to send him money to meet the cost of this year's coffee picking season. The payments have been delayed. He has not yet received the pay for the last harvest and this season's coffee berries are ripe. He has no money to finance the picking. He needs the money urgently or the coffee gets spoilt on the farm. The ghost of coffee time lingers on from one generation to the next!

My father stands disadvantaged in the coffee trade. At the café level, each kilogram of his coffee translates to over 200 cups of good coffee beverage. A cup of coffee in a German café, a cup of coffee goes for a minimum of 2 euros

24

(equivalent to 200 Kenya Shillings) or US$ 3 in the Starbuck's cafés that prevail in the United States of America. From the foregone example, it is evident that a kilogram of coffee at consumption level in Europe fetches 400 euros or Kshs 40,000 – over 2,000 times what my father receives in payment.

Millions of people drink a cup of coffee everyday. This demand for coffee has attracted many leading global food industries to invest in its manufacturing and distribution. The companies purchase tonnes of coffee from farmers in Africa. The companies rake huge profits, even as raw coffee prices remain depressed.

While all this happens, my father receives only US$ 0.17 for a kilogram of green coffee beans, at the retail end. Between my father and the roaster, layers of intermediaries strategically wait to skim off the gravy before it reaches the coffee producer. The intermediaries include the local elites who own the store and are able to provide some means of transport or small loans on condition that my father mortgages his coffee harvest at very low prices and/or repay the loans at usurious rates of interest. From the processor, the coffee lands into the waiting hands of private exporters who are mainly transnational corporations. These align the products to the demands of the importer. As with every intermediary, the exporter ensure that they buy the coffee at the lowest possible price and sell it at the maximum price they can get.

It would be prudent to follow the advice by Nestlé, one of the world's leading rosters and marketers of coffee, in its 1998 advertisement. The firm advised that: "Next time you enjoy a cup of Nescafe, stop and think about how more than 100 million people involved in the coffee growing industry have worked together to help you "open your day." We should go a step beyond thinking and ensure that the coffee trade elicits a win-win scenario where both the consumer and the producer will afford a smile.

www.ingramcontent.com/pod-product-compliance
Lightning Source LLC
Chambersburg PA
CBHW030854270326
41928CB00008B/1365